THE

JOURNEY

A SELECTION OF POETRY

By Julius P. Hall

Through my writing I give the world a view into my soul, my spirit, and my heart. I have always loved writing. Telling my story on paper instead of speaking it verbally. When writing, you can't be interrupted by someone trying to speak at the same time. You can truly express your thoughts and feelings and prayers to God. Hope you enjoy.

This book of poetry is dedicated to everyone who made me think, and who inspired me to write. Who believed in me when I didn't believe in myself. Who allowed me to love them and who loved me back. A special thanks to my favorite high school teachers, Ms. Ethel Lambert and Mr. Charles Brannan. To my coaches Joe Turner, Stanley Rivers and Ronald Puggy Jackson. To my children, Rockiea, Gabrielle, Akeem, Alexandria, Chance and Stardacia. To my wife, Tonia, for supporting my vision to write or do business. To my mothers, Louise Maner Tolbert, Brenda Harvey and Delores Screen. To my brother Ulysses for his wisdom and my brother, Johnny, for his strength. And to my entire class of 1981 from Tompkins High School in Savannah, Georgia.

"The biggest wall you have to climb is the one you built in your mind: Never let your mind talk you out of your dreams, trick you into giving up. Never let your mind become the greatest obstacle to success - All the advice in the world will never help you until you help yourself.

Your current situation is giving you an opportunity to reevaluate what you want. Don't carry your mistakes around with you, place them on the floor and use them as stepping stones to where you want to go.

Don't do less but still want more.

If you have a dream, fight for it. It's not about how many times you get rejected or you fall down or get beaten up. It's about how many times you stand, are brave and keep on going.

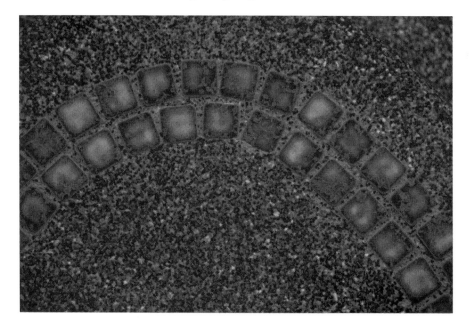

Most of the important things in the world have been accomplished by people who have kept on trying when there seemed to be no hope at all."

TABLE OF CONTENTS

Poems 1-10

WRITTEN: October 30, 1991 thru November 30, 1991

INSPIRATION/BACK STORY:

I wrote this group of poems as I sat in the Evans County Jail in Claxton, Georgia. I was feeling some kind of way after being tried and convicted, then sentenced to life in federal prison, my emotions were all over the place. I write what I feel, and over the course of these 30 days, I was feeling every emotion except happiness. As you read these 10 poems, you'll see that I was hurt, sad, disappointed, unsure, pissed off, and seeking God's favor. I felt like David in the bible, with all of his prayers and pleas to God in the book of psalms. I want people to see what I was feeling and I wanted God to come into that jail and rescue me. Many of those nights when I closed my eyes to sleep, I often asked God to not wake me the next morning.

I was ashamed and embarrassed. I felt like I had let so many people down. I cried a lot at night, but never in front of anyone. I didn't cry because I was scared of prison, I cried because I had failed. I cried because I was the golden boy, who was now looked at like the bronze boy. I cried because what I was putting my mom through, I cried because what my children would have to go through. I cried because I felt like I had to be the dumbest man in the world.

I ended up doing 21.5 years away from home. That time I did, I paid all of my debt. I live by this now: "once paid, a debt is no longer a debt."

Nobody can make me feel anything different. You can't embarrass me, shame me, or make me feel unworthy. My debt is paid here on earth. But I still owe God.

BUILDING A HOUSE

I found a man to build me a house the other day.
You might know him, He said his name is Jesus.

He told me not to worry. He built all his houses
on a foundation called God.

I had worries about the plumbing, but he
told me not to worry. He had a plumber named WISDOM.

I told him the blueprints looked kind of
complicated. He told me not to worry, he had a
blueprint reader named UNDERSTANDING.

The electrical work looked kind of backwards to me,
but he told me not to worry. The man who did the
electrical work has been doing it all of his life, you might
know him, his last name is KNOWLEDGE.

I was worried about the way the rood was being built, and
whether it would fall or cave in. But he told me not to worry.
the man hammering in the nails is from a family called
FAITH.

I had worries as to whether he would finish by the bank's
deadline, and he said to me, "don't worry, put God first and
then have. FAITH, KNOWLEDGE, WISDOM, and
UNDERSTANDING to
Believe" that he would be finished RIGHT ON TIME.

Date: 10-30-91
Evans County Jail
Claxton, GA
#1

ADDICTED TO GOD

When I woke this morning, I looked out
the window then said, "Boy, it's a beautiful
morning,"

My brother then asked me, "Are you on drugs
or something?"

I told him yes, I was on a drug, but
It was called GOD.

And I couldn't get any higher using
nothing else.

It never lets my high come down.
It's the best I've ever had.

It makes me feel like I can accomplish
Anything. It's not illegal to use.

I can get it from just about anywhere .
It gets me up in the mornings, and puts
me to sleep at night.

I can share it with everyone and never run out.
Last, but not least, it doesn't cost one
dime.

Date: 10-31-1991
Evans County Jail
Claxton, GA
#2

IF I NEVER SEE YOU AGAIN

Say that I was a man. That meant what I said, and said what I meant.

Say that I was a man that wouldn't compromise with the truth.

Say that I was a man that had lost God as a youth, and found him before it was too late.

Say that I loved my daughter more than I loved my own life.

Say that I cared about the oppressed, when no one else would.

Say that I was a friend to my friends, when my friends were not friends to me.

Say when I fought the system, I became tired and wanted to lay down, but I was too tired of the system to lay down.

Say that I cared about what happened to everybody else, before I cared about what would have happened to me.

Say that I never looked at anything one sided, because if God didn't say it, it had to be another side.

Say that I cared for everybody, even though everybody didn't care for me.

Don't say that the government did me wrong, just to promote their song.

Don't say that I was convicted because of the government's addiction to me.

Don't say that they lied on me and called it the truth.

Don't say that they swore to God on the witness stand, but was Satan in disguise.

Don't say that the Judge was unfair to me, he has to be judged on day also.

Don't say that the news media did me wrong; the only record played was the government's song.

Don't say "Oh God, Why Julius Hall?" I didn't question God when I got the call.

DATE: 11-9-1991
#3

JUST THE FACTS

I was investigated by Maxwell Smart and Barney Fife.
They told the grand jury a lie and I had to fight for my life.

They took me away to a country jail,
I couldn't find a soul to raise my bail.

I sat in jail four long, and hard days,
Would you believe I was there because of what someone had said?

They shamed my name and put me under the media's scope,
But no one bothered to tell them that I had no dope.

I felt my motions, and they all were denied,
All because the FBI had lied.

They wanted me to run, so they put me to the test.
I got out of jail and they placed me under house arrest.

I buckled down and waited four months,
While the FBI continued their witch hunt.

The government gave us all that it had discovered,
No substance at all, but three years it covered.

When the D.A. shifted to as the burden of proof,
My attorney almost went through the roof.

Court started on October the seventh,
The jury played "The Wheel of Fortune" on October eleventh.

We waited all day, and most of the night,
Then the jury decided to play "The Price Is Right."

I wanted to throw myself on the mercy of the court,

Then I remembered, it's God to whom I must report.

I went away bound and chained.
I was hurt, but GOD had gained.

When I read in the Bible, "There is nothing new under the sun."
I realized again that my Lord had won.

I know that he will free me, all in due time.
I believe he just wanted to get a hold of my mind.

Date: 11-10-1991
#4

COME AND SEE

We are not always guilty of everything you hear, come and
see.
They stack the jury with white people, we never have a jury
of our peers, come and see.

We are being used as the scapegoats for America's drug and
crime problems, come and see.
They want you to think so, but we don't make AK-47's, Uzi's
or
Machine Guns, come and see.

With guns and drugs, the court system, and prejudice, they've
created modern day legalized slavery, come and see.
The criminal justice system is being run by a bunch of Hitlers,
come and see.

They don't offer a Black addict rehabilitation, they only give him
incarceration, please come and see.
We're convicted by the media before court even starts, come and
see.

They have rules for us that don't apply to them, come and see.
The juror's fall to sleep, wake up and still convict us, come and see.

The lawyers assigned to defend us don't even practice criminal law,
come and see.
They give Blacks the maximum penalty, while Whites get a slap on
the wrist, come and see.

You get more time for a kilo of cocaine, than for killing 100
people, come and see.
The government is allowed to theorize, trick, bribe, lie and pay for
convictions, come and see.

We don't have the ships and planes to import drugs. Your Black
sons, brothers, and husbands are being taken from you for

something the White man controls or don't want to control, come and see.

They have sentencing guidelines that are written in Black and White. They hammer the Blacks and glue the Whites, come and see.

The laws and rules are so complicated, our lawyers need maps to figure them out. It's like the blind leading the blind, come and see.

They replaced the KKK with judges and juries, they replaced nigger and boy with guns and drugs. They replaced the plantations with prisons. They replaced racism with the criminal justice system. Please come and see.

You've got to come into the courtrooms, read between the lines, then tell me if their next plan isn't for you and me.

COME AND SEE, PEOPLE, COME AND SEE.

Date: 11-13-1991

#5

NOW THAT WE'VE PARTED

Now that we've parted,
I feel so broken hearted,
It was love at first sight,
Everything seemed so right.

But we should have known,
That one day it would be gone,
But we took a chance,
And relied on romance.

It was a difficult choice,
Can't you tell from my voice,
That I never really intended,
For our love to have ended.

Now I'm sick and I'm very weak,
I've not eaten, or gotten a wink of sleep,
I rode by your house a thousand times,
I just can't shake you from my mind.

I can't sleep at night,
Wondering if someone else is holding you tight,
We might not ever get back together,
But don't do my love like the wind does a feather.

I went my way and you went yours,
I cried all night and walked the beach shores,
Love is really hard and difficult to predict,
It's like an old alarm clock, you have to wind it
To make it tick.

You were my wife and we had a little girl,
I love you both more, than anything in this world.

DEDICATED TO Gabrielle D. Hall
In Memory of Tonya Wright Hall

Date: July 1988
Rewritten: 11-15-1991
#6

YOU ASKED HOW I'M FEELING

I've begun to feel just fine,
GOD has taken a load off of my mind,
I don't feel anymore pain,
Behind bars almost drove me insane.

I've gotten over feeling anything bad,
Even though I lost everything I had.
I was feeling down being away from my child,
Then GOD assured me, it's only for a little while.

I felt depressed after the jury's decision,
But GOD's handling the appeal with precision.
I felt kind of lonely, and missed my girlfriend,
I remembered people are only temporary, but with GOD
there is no end.

I felt homesick, doubtful, and sad,
GOD came to my rescue, and showed what I had.
I felt rejected by my father, it was like being stabbed by a
knife,
GOD told me to forgive him, and get on with my new
life.

I felt abandoned by my colleagues and many of my
friends,
Then GOD reminded me, it was only him that could my
broken heart mend.

I felt the judge was prejudice and very unfair,
Then GOD showed me his kingdom which was mine to

be shared.
I felt lies were told, that the jury refused to see.
Then GOD pointed out that the truth would set me free.

I now have faith, and I'm feeling really great.
Because I know GOD is carrying all my excess weight.

Date: 11-18-1991

#7

USE ME LORD

Use me Lord, to show that it's alright to be hated, branded and mocked,
As long as we know we're a member of your flock.

Use me Lord, to show that we all will be pushed and given the test,
But when it comes time to meet you, we'd better had given it our best.

Use me Lord, to show that it does not matter if we win or lose,
But when it comes down to God or the Devil, it's who we choose.

Use me Lord, to show that our roads will be rough and not always straight,
But we must travel them with you, for only you can open the pearly gates.

Use me Lord, to show that we will be tried and convicted for things we know nothing of,
But we must be patient, and have faith in our God above.

Use me Lord, to show that we will have to accept the slander and character assassination,
Because what matters overall, is our Godly association.

Use me Lord, to show that we will have troubles, along with pitfalls,
But God's the only one that can save us all.

Use me Lord, to show that the system is Unjust and we end up in jail,
But to get over this, we have to trust in a God that never fails.

Use me Lord, to show off pain, poverty and affliction,
But let me show also Lord that you can cure any addiction.

Use me Lord, to show there's gonna come an illness, in the form of a disease,
That will be as easy to catch as a cold from a sneeze.

Use me Lord, to show we're going to see backstabbers, pretenders and liars,
But we'll be alright, if we hang to God like a pair of grip pliers.

Use me Lord, to show that though we're living in the valley of the shadow of death,
It's not too late to be saved, if we haven't taken our last breath.

USE ME LORD, USE ME.

Date: 11-22-1991
#8

DON'T ASK ME ABOUT MY CASE

Don't ask me about my case, I won't ask you about
yours.
So when court starts, I won't have to worry about you
coming
In my backdoor.

If you ask me what I'm charged with, I'm going to tell
you a lie.
Hell, I just met you, how do I know you're not a
government spy.

You can tell me what you want, all about your case.
But when my court date comes, I don't want to see your
face.

The first thing you said was, "I know you, I'm from your
hometown."
Right then and there, I could see that you were a
government clown.

You persisted all night trying to bleed me for
information.
But you'd better stay out of my business, before there's a
Murder investigation.

You showed me all your paperwork, trying to prove
you're one of us.
But I know I've seen your face somewhere, was it on a
police drug bust?

I finally had to tell you to stay away from me and out of my cell.
Because when I looked in your eyes, I saw the devil and lots of hell.

You left me alone, and moved on to the next man.
Then I thought to myself, "Boy does the government have
A diabolical plan?"

I walked down the hall, and heard you giving Rick the same line.
If he knew what I know, he'd better shut up, or he'll be doing plenty of time.

I write this poem for those of us who might go to jail,
And run into a snitch, before you get out on bail.

LAST NOTE: after making bond, be careful who you meet,
They're not only in the jail, their in the streets.

Date: 11-22-19991
#9

AN INSIDE VIEW

They arrested me, my sister and my brother.
All their commotion nearly killed my mother.
My sister Cecilia was surprisingly strong.
For she knew all along, she did nothing wrong.

I got depressed and lost twenty-one pounds,
All because the government ran the wrong ship aground.
My friend Diana was very upset,
Because they accused me of drugs, instead of a bet.

Gabrielle lost her mom, the system took her dad,
Two very good people, who wouldn't be sad.
Bernard jump up, hooped and hollered,
For everywhere we went, the government followed.

The government played with our lives like bigtime stockbrokers,
They arrested my brother who was only a smoker.
Lamar was angry, but Nay felt betrayed,
People who he thought to be his friends, recorded what he said.

James was arrested on a South Miami Street,
This poor guy fixed cars, to make ends meet.
He didn't understand, is what made him so mad.
Why was he arrested for something he never had?

A guy named "Jo-Jo" came and told a lie,
He told the jury I was his inside spy.
He also told them he had sold me dope,
Six jurors were asleep, six were woke.

An atheist named "Red" came back from the dead,
How could a jury believe a word that he said?
I often wondered, if Calvin should be blamed,
Or was I just a picture, the government wanted framed?

I wasn't allowed to explain my whole case,
Guilty was all over the judge's face.
When court was over my sister was set free,
But I was found guilty, how could this be?

No one can replace the time I am to lose.
But God came to my cell, and gave me his spiritual tools.

Date: 11-30-1991
#10

Poems 11-22

WRITTEN: 12-01-1991 - 01-14-1992

INSPIRATION/BACK STORY:

These 12 poems were written during my first christmas and new years in prison. Being away from my loved ones and friends during these two holidays can be very depressing. I write in my feelings a lot. I also write to send a message to someone. During this period I was mad at the world, but especially at my friends who had let me down. I was mad at my trial judge. I was mad at my roommate bernard, I was mad at people for not seeing what I saw in an unjust system of law. 99% of my poetry rhymes. I don't know why, but it does. I was mad with my city, Savannah, Georgia. There were no happy feelings while I wrote this group of 12 poems. I was sending a message to everyone. I write very little poetry that is fiction. Most of what I write is true, at least to me.

WHAT CHRISTMAS REALLY MEANS

Have we forgotten what Christmas is all about?
Most people still think it's money, gifts, cards and clout?
Jesus was born far away in a manger,
God brought him here, to warn us of a danger.

He walked the plains and traveled rough lands,
For God had given him our eternal plans.
He fed the hungry and healed those that were ill.
He had twelve disciples to help do GOD'S will.

He wouldn't give in to temptations made by SATAN,
For he knew at the end of his journey the Lord would be
waiting.
They found him guilty, then nailed him to the cross.
God planned it this way so we would not be lost.

They took him down and placed him in a tomb,
He was born again, But not from the womb.
That's enough to keep me focused right,
Because Christmas is all about JESUS CHRIST.

Date: 12-1-1991
#11

WHENEVER YOU GET THE TIME

I'm Sorry I bothered you, But
Whenever you get the time, write me
Whenever you get the time, call me
Whenever you get the time, come see me
Whenever you get the time, do what I asked you to
Whenever you get the time, read what I wrote you
Whenever you get the time, try feeling what I feel

Whenever you get the time, go where I've been
Whenever you get the time, think about me
Whenever you get the time, dream about me
Whenever you get the time, remember what I told you
Whenever you get the time, remember the things we did
Whenever you get the time, remember what we shared

Whenever you get the time, remember where I'm at
Whenever you get the time, dream impossible dreams
Whenever you get the time, pick up your bible and read
Whenever you get the time, PRAY TO GOD FOR
MORE TIME.

Date: 12-02-1991
#12

TO GOOD A FRIEND

I know I haven't been a perfect friend,
But who was there when you were near the end?
I haven't been the greatest friend, but who
Did you call when it was a rule you'd bend?

I know I wasn't your toughest friend,
But when you were in trouble, I was the first to defend.
I probably wasn't your most trustworthy friend,
But for something important, who would you send?

I know I was your most excellent friend,
But you'd have to admit, I would never pretend.
I know I wasn't your closest friend, but,
When you lost your loved ones, didn't I attend?

I know I wasn't your very best friend,
But when you had not a dollar, I gave you ten.
I don't know if you consider me a special friend,
But I guess not, you never wrote it with a pen.

So friends we are now, friends we won't always be.
I can't depend on my friends, but my friends always
depended on me.

Date: 12-02-1991
#13

SENTENCING DAY

Don't worry about me, I'll be alright,
For GOD is with me day and night.
If you think my sentence is a bit too long,
Don't cry, GOD corrects everything that is wrong.

The judge won't be playing "Let's Make a deal,"
But "I got you nigger, under my heels."
If the sentence isn't "LIFE," I'd be surprised,
Justice for blacks don't come from these guys.

I will take it to my Lord for he knows how I feel,
Before the judge had finished, GOD was working my appeal.
It might take a while before I get out,
But I will, for I have no doubt.

Even though we know the system isn't fair,
Just pick up a bible, it tells you who cares.
Don't sit and think that your prayers didn't work,
The system is ran by Satan and his clerks..

The judge is playing God by giving life,
When his day comes, it'll be filled with strife.
The judge will ask me, "Do I have anything to say?"
Yes your honor; "God didn't tell me this was Judgment Day."

Date: 12-04-1991
Sentencing Date: 12-06-1991 #14

STAND UP BLACK PEOPLE

They chained us up and beat us with their whips,
They held auctions and sold us into slave ships.
We called them master and sometimes boss,
They taught us their language and our heritage we lost.

They hid the Bible and every other book,
We were only allowed to work for them and cook.
They decided to give us a few civil rights,
It was fine in the daytime, but they wore sheets at night.

We started to speak up against this evil man,
People started to listen, so he developed another plan.
He made new laws and rearranged the courts,
But we couldn't file a charge, not even a tort.

Along came a man, we all know as King.
Hoover took his life with a bullet's ring.
About the same time, there was a President named
Kennedy,
He talked the truth and received the death penalty.

Twenty years later, we moved into a new era.
Reagan and Bush became the new Pharaohs.
So just sit back and look from side to side.
Their plan is for you, and you cannot hide.

They used to call you "Boy," just for fun.
Until they replaced the "Boy," and gave you a gun.
They use to hang you from a tree by a rope,
Until they replaced that, with a powder they call dope.

So wake up Black people and smell what's cooking,
Before the next thing you know, it's you they're booking.
Stop looking for that four leaf clover.
They can't ride your back, if you're not bending over.

Date: 12-04-1991
#15

Footnote:
A Tort: is a civil wrong.
Pharaohs: was the King in the Bible who ordered all
male Jewish children, 2 years old and younger be killed, in
an attempt to kill Jesus.

THE JUDGE'S BOOK

They play with words and they play with numbers,
But someday people, their system will crumble..
Life is life and it means til my death,
But the Lord will take me up, before my last breath.

I looked at the D.A, I observed the judge,
No place in my sentencing would they budge.
I couldn't understand how long it took.
Until the judge requested, a review of "the book".

Inside it he turned from page to page,
But only GOD gives life, no matter what this book said.
It suggested time, and contained the rules,
But for black people, it only gave the blues.

It clearly shows that our laws are not right,
It gives death to blacks, and vacations to whites.
I can't blame the judge, society thinks it's progress,
But the judge took my side, and he blamed Congress.

As my lawyer told the judge, he thinks they're wrong,
They must be deaf and blind, GOD and I knew it all
along.
When he read my sentence, my head I shook,
For the judge read my sentence, from the devil's book.

Date: 12-06-1991
#16

40

SAVANNAH, GA

Savannah is a city that creates its own trouble,
They blame the blacks when the crime rate doubles.
Savannah is a city, in need of much luck,
After the southside, the city sucks.

You can blame some of it on the thieves in city hall,
They gave blacks a basketball, and built white's a mall.
It's a city where the people are easily misled,
They accept anything, even a bullet in the head.

If you're white, you're called a cracker,
You get anything you want without a backer.
If you're black, you're called a nigger,
You don't vote, you never speak up, but you pull a
trigger.

It's a city where the people have lost their backbone,
The weak are still there, but the strong are gone.
It's a city where some, are hooked on power,
They'll steal your towel, while you're in the shower.

Savannah is a city, that needs resuscitating,
But at the moment, it's regurgitating.
Savannah, Is a city you need not visit,
Just stay on the highway, Don't take it's exit.

Date: 12-09-1991
#17

41

REFLECTIONS OF YOU

When I think of the love you've shown me,
In my eyes I begin to cry,
And when I think of the strength you've given to me,
It's more than enough to get by.

When I think of the courage you've instilled in me,
I feel I can accomplish anything,
And when I think of the wisdom you've shared with me,
I'm better prepared for what tomorrow might bring.

When I think of the time you've given me,
By you never leaving my side.
I begin to think of the knowledge you've given me.
To help with the things I must decide.

When I think of the joy you've given me,
By doing the things I've asked.
I start to think of the feeling you'll get,
When God pays you my tax.

When I think of the happiness you've given me,
By means of your support.
I begin to think of the skills you've taught me,
For the things in my life to sort.

I can't even put into words, how I feel about you,
But I'll make it as simple as I can. How about, "I love
you?"

DEDICATED TO MY MOMS
LOUISE TOLBERT & DELORES SCREEN

Date: 12-17-1991
#18

BEING A POLICEMAN

Most policemen will do anything to further their careers,
Some go as far, as to lie on the innocent, and even on
their peers.

Some policemen have no respect for the uniform,
They're too busy kissing butt, or trying to outperform.

Some know their jobs, others know only the badge,
Of all the policemen I knew, most only bragged.

Some drove patrol cars, and a few rode motors,
What the public don't know, is that they all have quotas.

Thefts, rapes, fights, and accidents are par for the course,
But murder was the crime we hated to ride the most.

Child molestations and suicides were every now and then,
Drugs and domestics were something on which you
could depend.

After a full day on the job, you're bound to be under
stress,
You get a little relief when you can take off your
bulletproof vest.

While doing your job you hold many titles, like
"Peacemaker,"
"Protector," and "Advisor."
You feel proud and honored about your job, until you get
chewed out
By your shift Supervisor.

Nothing feels as good, as when you've helped another person,

Or when you've helped the less fortunate deal with desertion.

Some wanted the authority, because the pay wasn't superb,

But when I went to work, my job was to serve.

(Former Police Officer)
Date: 01-05-1992
#19

THE BIG PICTURE II

With the Jivens gang in jail, who's doing the shootin?
Ah, you know who it is, for you're doing the rootin.
The New Year came in, with a very loud bang,
Three were left dead, who's the leader of this gang?

People with guns are a dangerous thing,
Blacks don't make them, but to their pockets they cling.
Drugs have become "the order of the day,"
It's not grown in America, but we have it as we may.

Anti-drug groups are starting up, and they're
marching in the streets.
I've begun to wonder, is this where the first
Book and the last book of the Bible begin to meet?

Little do they know, that they can hold their breath,
For they're walking the streets, just for their health.
Our political leaders are to whom they need voice this
concern.
For if we don't stop the importation, this country will
burn.

Our leaders today, are truly a mystery,
The only thing on their minds is making history.

Date: 01-07-1992
#20

PRISON

It's a place to think, a place to dream, a place
To wonder and a place to reflect on "what if."
It is a place to laugh, a place to cry, and for me,
The law has made it a place to die.

It is a place to forgive, a place to forget the past,
And a place to hope for the future.
It is also a place to hurt, a place of pain, and if you
Don't have a strong mind, it's a place to drive you insane.

It's a place to sort your true friends, your real family,
And a place to test someone's love.
It is a place of peace, a place of rest,
and a place to, finally get a lot of things off of your
chest.

It is a place to meet evil men, a place to meet good men,
And also a place to meet innocent men.
It is a place to hear drug stories, a place to hear crime
stories, but most of all, a place to hear some great
testimonies.

It is a place to loose religion, a place to find religion,
And a place to seek much more religion.
It's a place to say some prayers, a place to hear some
prayers, and a place to get some prayers answered.

Date: 01-14-1992
#21

THE LURES

The lures of Satan look mighty fine.
Disguised in gold, cars and wine.
The lures of flesh is not the least,
It looks as if a wonderful feast.

The covet of money is not the most,
For in pursuit Mammon is host,
All these things are Satan's deception,
Eagerly awaiting your reception.

The roads I travel were filled with strife,
Many times nearly costing me my life,
The devil will give you many clues,
But your soul in hell are his dues.

The devil will go to many extremes,
Even tempting in your dreams,
What I have forgiven, GOD was told,
But I was forgiven a Thousand fold.

For Christ has powers beyond belief,
When you are burdened, he gives you relief,
Although I've suffered endless pain,
My humble prayers were not in vain.

But though his grace I was spared,
To do his will for only he cared,
All these things were not my damnation,
For it all ended in my salvation.

Written By: Clayton Tanner
Date: 11-30-1991

Location: Claxton, GA #22

Poems 23-29

WRITTEN: 01-15-1979 - 06-20-1983

INSPIRATION/BACK STORY:

These 7 poems were all written during my high school years and my puppy love years. My first experience with love. The first woman I lived with at age 17. The first time that understood that love is the most powerful force in the universe. I've been a fool for love ever since. You'll see why in the poems to come later in this book. I can write about anything, but love is my best topic. These 7 poems shaped my love life. There are three things that we chase for all of our life; God, money and love.

I was young and these poems show just how young I was.

FALLING IN LOVE

Falling in love is an easy thing,
Falling in love makes you want to sing.
It's something that is easy to spot,
You have the key, so put it in the slot.

Telling her is where you get the pain,
If you don't know how, it'll drive you insane.
You'll stay up at night thinking of the girl,
Who you hope to love most in the world.

You ask her dad for her hand,
And then he tells you where he stands.
When he tells you no, you want to fight,
But you hold it off with all your might.

Then you ask her mother for her consent,
And she asks you, "how you gonna pay the rent?."
You both decide to run away,
Loving each other more day by day.

But it doesn't matter when you're in love,
Because you're always watched from above.

Date: 01-15-1979
#23

MY MAN

He's someone who I can depend,
To hold me when I'm near the end.
He understands yes or no,
Bad feelings he does not show,
When I'm in the need for care,
He's always there with something to share.
And when he comes with bad news,
I'm there! So how can we lose?
When I see he's out of line,
He can't help that he's fine.
When I need him, I never fear to call.
By the way, he's Julius Hall.

Date: 02-03-1980
#24

FEELINGS

This is something from above,
That some confuse with love.

It's from the bottom of your heart,
To the top of your head,
Usually, this is where, the tears
Begin to shed.
This is something you have to prepare,
To give away or even share.
It can catch you before you look,

And if it does, you know you're hooked.
Feelings can make you laugh or smile,

If you want it like love, you'll walk a country mile.

Date: 02-25-1980
#25

TANIA

When I'm with you, I feel so good,
And when we kiss, my heart turns to wood.
Why I want you, I haven't found out,
But I need you and there's no doubt.
When I'm sick, you are my cure,
That's how I know, this love is pure,
And when it turns from day to night,
I can't wait to see your sight.
In the mornings when I wake,
I think of you and the joy you make.
And when I look into your eyes,
I see that you tell no lies.
You never spoil or make a mess,
That's how I know that you're blessed.
I bet on you and won big bucks,
Now I know, you are my luck.

Date: 07-10-1980
#26

55

MARGUERITE

What it is, I do not know.
If it's love, I want to be sure.
You make me happy and you make me "Feel,"
But don't fall in Love until it's real.

You touched my heart, you touched my soul.
Let's keep it this way until we're old.
I once was out and feeling down,
But you pulled me in, before I hit the ground.

To my life, you bring sunshine.
That's why I look ahead, and not behind.
I know exactly where I want to be,
As close to you, as the air is to me.

Skin to skin, lip to lip,
Arm to arm and hip to hip.
If you want anymore there's always room,
But if you don't, just pick up a broom.

Date: 08-11-1982
#27

WHO ME?

I'm five foot nine,
All fine.
Said, who gives a damn,
I weight a hundred and thirty,
Built sturdy.
Said, I am always clean,
Never dirty.
I got a girlfriend,
That fights to the end.
So when it comes to me,

She's ready to defend.
I said be, be
What you want to be.
But when it comes to my stuff,

Don't mess with me.
Said my skin is black,

I catch "Don't F with me" attacks,
So when I catch one,
You better back, back.

Date: 11-26-1982
#28

LEAVING LOVE

Leaving your love is hard to do,
Even for me and even for you.
When you find that love is in your heart,
The next thing you know, you're breaking apart.
You say it's wrong, but it's better,
So you write to her, a heartbreak letter.
It's hard to look her in her eyes,
But when you do she always cries.
I write this poem, for those who choose,
To fall in love and always lose.
Only I, know where to begin,
Because I never lose, I always win.

Date: 06-20-1983
#29

Poems 30-40

WRITTEN: 02-10-1992 - 03-19-1993

INSPIRATION/BACK STORY:

Most of my poetry centers on love, but during this time I was dealing with a whole lot. Friends not showing up, people quitting and giving up on me, feeling hopeless, and then some days feeling like I wanted to expose this unjust criminal justice system to the world. Then my brother, Johnny, sent me 3 poems to add to my collection.

People knew that i wrote poetry and would often send me their writings to see if I like theirs. In this book of poetry there are 3 - 5 poems that I didn't write. I believe johnny has 3 poems in here, my friend from the Evans County Jail, Clayton Tanner has 1 and I think my daughter has 1. All the other poems are my original work.

NEVER GIVE UP, NEVER QUIT

I was taught to "Never give up and never quit,"
For if I did, I would become a dumb nitt-witt.
I was taught, "Keep on trying, you'll get there one day,"
Work hard, put God first, and you will see your big
payday.

I was taught, "You can be anything you want to be,"
Learn, Plan, and React, Then one day you'll see.
I was taught, "do it today, don't wait on tomorrow,"
For tomorrow's are always full of sorrow.

So when you're fighting the Devil, don't throw in the
towel,
Fight hard, God will save you before the eleventh hour.
And if you think you're dead, or about to check out,
Just remember what Jesus 'dying 'was all about.

So never give up and never ever quit,
Even though your life might be sunk in a pit.
Everything that happens is not always right,
But God promised he'd come, like a thief in the night.

If you leave God out, and still come to a conclusion,
The only thing you'll have is one of the devil's illusions.
I've learned that "Life isn't over until your heart stops
beating,"
If you quit before then, it's God you're cheating.

Date: 02-10-1992 #30

MY DARLING UNEIDA

Sorry I can't send a card, sorry I can't send you roses,
Because for you, if I could, I'd part the red sea like
Moses.
I'm sorry I can't get to you, I'm sorry I can't get home,
But first chance I get, I'm going to take you to Rome.

I've finally come to the conclusion,
That you're not an illusion.
So I'm ready to live my life,
But only with you as my wife.

You're never weak, but always very strong,
With you in my life, how can I go wrong?
So wait a little while and I'll be back,
To give you everything in the world, I know you'd like.

I can't be there with you, but I pray I'm in your thoughts,
To me that is more important, than anything I could've
bought.
If I didn't know before, I know now the meaning of
love,
It came to me through you, "MY SNOW WHITE
PRECIOUS DOVE."

Another way to tell you, that it's you that I love,
Is, "I want to be as close to you "as five fingers in a
glove"
I hope that this poem, can take the place of flowers,

Regardless of that, I'll be thinking of you 24 hours.

Date: 02-18-1992
#31

"THANK YOU PRESIDENT BUSH"

Thank you President Bush, for violating my rights,
God's arrival on Earth is now in our sights.
Thank you President Bush, for your help in destroying
my people,
Thomas and Powell are only helping you remain a
"keeper."

Thank you President Bush for killing the quotas,
You showed us through that you're another P.W. Botha.
Thank you President Bush, for praising Darryl Gates,
We know what kind of people are allowed through the
White House Gates.

Thank you President Bush, for helping spread AIDS,
Magic Johnson had to catch it before you listened to
what the people said.
Thank you President Bush, for my life of oppression and
pain,
Reagan started the lies, then you took us down the drain.

Thank you President Bush, for knocking me to my knees,
This is your period to rule, so do as you please.
Thank you President Bush, for revealing your true self,
But, I'd already read about you, from that book on my
shelf.

Thank you President Bush, for creating for the people
jobs,
It's because of you, we have to sell dope and rob.
Thank you President Bush for having your line "Read my

Lips,"
While we were busy reading them, a knife in our backs you slipped.

Thank you President Bush for your "New World Order,"
If I had to pay you for it, I'd need change for a quarter.
Thank you President Bush, for absolutely nothing at all,
While we are catching Hell, you were out stroking a golf ball.

Date: 05-08-1992
#32

ON MY DYING BED

When I get sick and I'm about to check out,
Will anyone remember what my living was about?
Will it be my heart, cancer, or will I die of old age?
In the book of life, will I have turned the last page?

Will you still love me, hate me, or give a damn?
Will it be you that will bury me, or will it be Uncle Sam?
Will you pray for me to go to Heaven, because I was so
swell?
Or will you pray for me, eternal Hell?

Will you tell lies, the truth, or a little of each?
Or will I be the topic whenever you speak?
When I was with you, I was always your hero,
But when I'm gone, will you grade me a zero?

I'll try to envision how the hereafter will be,
No more sin, just peace, and I'll finally be free.
When I'm laying there on my dying bed,
Will you remember what I wrote, or anything I said?

Date: 08-16-1992
#33

65

THE FINAL CALL FOR FREEDOM, JUSTICE AND EQUALITY

When was the last time you had any freedom, justice and equality?
No, I didn't say anything about sex, violence and iniquity.
Freedom: The ability to move or do, come and go, without being hindered.
Answer: Not since your soul to the Devil you've surrendered.

Justice: A system of rules and laws that govern a society.
Answer: Not since the Paleman took over as your deity.
Equality: To be given a fair chance and to be treated equal.
Answer: Not until Judgment Day, which is the final sequel.

Some seem to think we can get all this through government administration,
Some seem to think we can get all this through government legislation.
With Martin Luther King we thought we could get it through demonstration,
With Thurgood Marshall we hoped for it through litigation.

We can have it, if we prepare for Judgment Day through careful preparation,
Of if we register our names in "The book of life" through registration
And if we meditate in prayer through meditation.

Freedom, justice and equality is (Allah's) God's salvation. These things are represented by the moon, the sun and the stars.

Come together Black people and let's take back what's ours.

An old saying was, "Together we stand, Divided we fall." Wake up blind, dead and dumb Black people, this is the final call.

Date: 11-24-1992
#34

THE BLOOD AND THE CRIPS

This is a poem about a bunch of boys,
Who play with guns like they are toys.
One group wears blue and the other one wears red,
Wear the wrong colors and you could end up dead.

You can't call one your Blood, or the other your Cuz.
For if you do, your name could quickly change to was.
You can't call one slob, or the other a crab.
Just speak and keep going, to stay out of the coroner's lab.

Disruption and destruction is the only thing they know,
Rudeness and bad manners, the only emotions they show.
Most are serving life, one I know is doing a triple,
Before he killed, he would snort powder and drink some ripple.

Violence and bloodshed leaves most of us stunned,
To the these young thugs, it's just another day of fun.
Savage, is the way I'd like to think of them least,
But how can I, when they're living the life of a beast.

They kill each other, but put the enemy on the back burner,
They must not have read the story of Nat Turner.
From all I've seen, they're all a bunch of pranksters,
Who believe in their minds, they're really gangsters.

Wake up guys, and just look at what you're doing,

Genocide, is what you fools have got brewing,
It's not your fault, and not even your plan,
But it's all the ideal of that evil pale man.

Date: 11-29-1992
#35

THE RESURRECTION OF MALCOLM X

Brother Malcolm was a born leader and a humble man,
For our Black people he delivered Allah's master plan,
He was born and raised at the bottom of the social heap,
He knew that what White America reaped, so shall they
also weep.
Malcolm left school to lead a life of crime,
But had a spiritual rebirth to the Nation of Islam while
doing time.

When Malcolm started his life of crime, his name was
Detroit Red,
But once he found the N.O.I., "X was in, and Detroit
was dead.

This was his message to the Black man,
"Stop depending on White America and take a stand,"
When he talked about this unjust White race,
Never once did a smile come upon his face.

Not all White men are born of the Devil,
But eventually he will dig his grave with his own shovel.
White America has kept us in bondage as a tradition,
Their only desire was to keep us in this miserable
condition.

With over four hundred years of slavery, White America
is in our debt,
And if White America refuses to pay, they will surely
regret.
Ultimately, the Muslim in America will gain control,
White America if you don't change, your's will be a

horrible story told.

But Malcolm did not bring this message alone,
For most of Black America wants to leave, to go back to
a land of their own.

For any Black Cause, Malcolm would show up to fight,
So why have we, the 20th Century brothers, lost our
sight?
Before Malcolm died, he went on a pilgrimage to Mecca,
Because he knew his life was soon to end in racist
America.

For he left Mecca with a peaceful coexistence vision,
And still America did not respect the N.O.I. decision,
Black America, although Malcolm is gone,
His struggle for freedom, justice and equality must go on.

U.S.P. Atlanta
#36

MANDATORY SLAVERY

For conspiracy the government needs no evidence
But for all Black brothers this is a serious offense
The government is stirring in our people a sense of no hope,
The same government is responsible for all the dope.

We're appointed lawyers that don't want our case,
Because the government is charging us with cocaine base.
The government came out with its mandatory guideline,
It doesn't affect them, so they are fine.

The Constitution was never written for the Black man,
Not even when George Bush saw Clarence Thomas as his biggest fan.
Thomas Jefferson said "All men should be treated the same,"
This was only his way of gaining fame.

When we enter the courtroom the prosecutor is in control,
For us Black brothers, is the worst story told.
The jurors are usually mostly all White,
Before we get started, we've already lost the fight.

Our lawyers tell us that "We can win on appeal,"
With all those White judges this can't be real.
Our Black brothers are getting life, with no chance for parole,
By a justice system that's totally out of control.

This system says, we're well adapted to be slaves,
But now we'll fight to our graves.
America has robbed us of the knowledge of self,
To our cry for justice it seems to be deaf.

How can we be talking about the same God,
When he hasn't and won't, spare the black man the rod?

Written By: Johnny J. Hall
Date: 07-12-1992
Location: U.S.P. Atlanta
#37

EXCEPTANCE

ALLAH works throughout his creation with mercy and justice, "repent,"
For this reason THE HONORABLE ELIJAH MUHAMMAD was sent.

As we go through life, we sometimes set a goal.
But the truth of ALLAH must always remain in our soul

ALLAH'S message is merciful, the truth, and the light.
So not for spoil or gain, but for this cause do we fight.

For Pharaoh was arrogant, and ALLAH taught him a lesson.
So has America disrespected ALLAH, with their blessing.

If you go through life against ALLAH'S will, there will always be a bend,
Because the dangers of indiscipline, disputes, loss of courage, usually brings a selfish end.

Those with faith are like the seeing, and those without are like the blind.
For ALLAH'S most glorious gift is the QURAN, denounce sin but be gentle and kind.

Signs and favors will guide a man to ALLAH, but arrogance will mislead.
Be faithful in intent and action, to evil and falsehood take heed.

Service of ALLAH is duty to man, and ALLAH'S glory

is declared in his creation,
So guard your words and avoid evil, because his truth is
his revelation.

Be not impatient, THE HEREAFTER IS CERTAIN, let
us not go astray but wait.
Revelation warns against evil, and guides to good
everlastings to us with faith.

Written By: Johnny J. Hall
Date: 08-19-1992
Location: U.S.P. Atlanta
#38

SLAVERY, SUFFERING & DEATH

You beat us, you killed us, and you made our hearts ache,
The more cruel you'd be, the more we'd take.
Then one day, when we finally got tired,
We stood up together thinking your time had expired.

You gave in here and gave a little there,
But still loading us down with more than we could bare.
Little did we know, it was just one of your tricks,
It was like going to a party and getting slipped a mick.

Of all the bridges we've built, and the roads we've laid,
For over 400 years, we've never gotten paid.
How could any of this be deemed justified,
With all the black people that have died?

Everything you said we had to obey,
Or you'd put your whip to our backs and have it your
way.
For years we cried, "Oh God send us a guide."
But everytime God would send one, we'd run and hide.

YOU brainwashed us into loving a white Jesus who was
divine,
And this is where I believe, we lost our damn minds.
I guess we would call it, "The era of lost sight,"
Until along came Louis Farrakhan carrying the light.

We were wrong not to fight, when told to withhold,
It's time for our hearts to grow hard and cold.
We must stand as one, showing that enough is enough,

We're not putting up with no more of this Devil's stuff.
I guess I'm just one who will always complain,
Because I'm with the old cliche', no pain no gain.
You might call me crazy, or you might call me bold,
But I already know that you must win, to get the gold.

You control all the money and nothing is made simple,
Want to know more, just read "Secrets of the Temple."
One thing's certain, in the white man's pursuit of wealth,
Blacks have only gotten slavery, suffering, & death.

Date: 02-04-1992
Location: U.S.P. LOMPOC
#39

"I'M DYING OF A BROKEN HEART"

Oh Father, Oh Father, is it meant for me to suffer?
Nothing is getting easier, it seems everything is tougher.
Is it meant for me to hurt and feel as I feel?
Is this just a nightmare or is this really real?

I feel so empty and I've been doing some crying,
I'm down so low right now, that I feel like dying.
My life was fine, when it was your love I had focused,
But now will you kill our love, by just saying Hocus
Pocus?

My heart, my heart, Oh Lord, How it hurts,
I can't go to sleep and I don't want to work.
I know that life is full of its ups and downs,
But why do I have to feel like a sad face circus clown?

You found somebody else and he's nice it seems,
But the question is: What did our love really mean?
You took more than just love away from me,
You took my heart, my soul and my spirit you couldn't
see?

I'm confined to bed and I haven't been eating,
Please, Lord stop my heart from beating.
If our love is to be saved, It'll need a jump start,
Oh Lord, Oh Lord, Heal my broken heart.

Date: 03-19-1993
Location: F.C.I. Talladega #40

Poems 41-49

WRITTEN: 04-16-1993 - 10-01-1993

INSPIRATION/BACK STORY:

This was my "I'm tired of this b.s. happening in our community" period. My "I see it and I have to address it" period. My "I'm pissed off now" period. I wanted to tell everyone off. I wanted the world to hear me. I was tired of being lied to and forgotten about. Everything I saw that was out of balance, I wrote about. Even to president bush. I wanted my former friends to know that I was over it, that I didn't need them anymore, that my crying days were over. I was in my feelings, so I wrote about it. Lol.

FOR YOU

You touched my heart and you touched my soul,
You warmed my spirits and brought me in from the cold.
There are so many beautiful thoughts I have of you,
You've never once refused to do what I asked you to.

I should've seen it in your lovely eyes, or in your "I love
you" smile,
So before I die, for you, shall I do, something truly
worthwhile.
I love you baby, more than you could ever think,
When I think of you, I see lovely shades of pink.

Please don't hate me for not marrying you when I had
the chance,
But if it be God's will, I shall ask you for the first dance.
Oh baby, I want to share with you all my dreams,
I want to make your coffee, and be your sugar and cream.

Then I want to wash your back and comb your hair,
I want our love to be known throughout this hemisphere.
I want to take you here, and I want to take you there,
I want our love to be the symbol, by which to be
compared.

I want to do for you what I never did,
I want to show you the love I always hid.
I want to call you darling, sweetheart, baby and honey,
I want to give you something more precious than money.

Date: 04-16-1993
#41

80

"NO THANK YOU MR. HOG"

The hog is known all over as pig and swine,
It's not a friend of yours and it's not a friend of mine.
You'll find it is forbidden to be eaten in the Quran,
I won't eat it, I'd rather be beaten like Rodney King with
a baton.

You'll also find that it is the same meat of which the
Bible spoke,
Leave it alone, to avoid a heart attack or a stroke.
Don't give me any ribs and I surely don't want any pig
tails,
I'd rather spend my life as a bum on the rails.

Don't give me bacon, no neck bones or no pig feet,
You'll only be making a place for me six feet deep.
The male hog will watch his female hog have sex,
With every other pig, from Arnold to Tex.

The hog is known as the supreme germ carrier,
The more filth it eats, it seems to get merrier.
How could anyone serve or eat this forbidden meal?
Is the hog a sign of Satan or is it his seal?

If you believe all the good things that's said about pork,
I guess you also believe, that babies are delivered by the
stork.
If you still think the hog is good and you feel secure,
Remember the hog will eat anything, even manure.

The pig carries with it, 21 serious diseases,

That attacks your body and does as it pleases.
The last thing I'll say about eating the hog,
Is you'd be much better off, eating the family dog.

Date: 04-21-1993
Location: F.C.I. Talladega
#42

"CASUALTIES OF WAR"

A soldier is wounded and to the ground he falls,
If the wound is bad, it is to his God he calls,
We're all apart of this devastating battle,
It's like who is next to be slaughtered of the cattle.

We're divided on this and we're divided on that,
It's like going to home plate, without a bat.
Frederick Douglas once said "Progress and Struggle go
hand in hand."
So we have to be prepared to die for that for which we
stand.

In every war, each side must have a plan,
If your strategy is weak, you could lose every man.
Everyone must understand that they're not to be caught,
Winning doesn't matter, as much as how you fought.

You have to be ready to both lead and follow,
For there's no such thing as a tomorrow.
No matter what your goal or if it has a fallacy,
Casualties of war is not a quality.

NOTE: FALLACY IS A FALSE IDEA, OR
DIFFERENT REASONING.

Date: 04-24-1993
Location: F.C.I. Talladega
#43

THE MEASURE OF YOUR SUCCESS

You can only learn so much by attending college,
So pride is surely the enemy of knowledge.
Sometimes we're blind to the consequences to come,
So anger is certainly the enemy of wisdom.

If you can't wait, you could lose your existence,
So greed is surely the enemy of patience.
When you tell a lie, you should lose every tooth,
So falsehood is surely the enemy of truth.

This one shouldn't be a hard point to ponder,
Is infamy the enemy of what we call honor?
The meaning of love, is not push and shove,
So shouldn't we call hate, the enemy of love?

Some people tell lies in order to achieve,
The bigger the lie, the more likely it is to be believed.
The strong usually takes advantage of the weak,
So on the day of judgment, you'll get what you seeked.

The air keeps the record of your words and deeds,
So watch what you plant, you'll be judged by your seeds.
Success is not knowledge, nor is it gold by the pound.
Success is getting up, one more time than you fall down.

Date: 05-04-1993
Location: F.C.I. Talladega
#44

"WRITE BACK SOON"

Almost every week, I took out my pen and pad,
And I wrote to you, about the things I thought we had.
Ten day would pass, then there would be twenty,
How much time do you need? I thought a month to be
plenty.

Monday thru Friday and nothing from you, but I sweated
the mail,
Did the me you knew die, when I came to jail?
No postcard, no birthday card and no sign of a letter,
Hurts like hell now, but things have got to get better.

If I did something wrong, please let me know,
If I can't correct it, I'll bother you no more.
It's not money I want, although some will do,
But what matters to me, is my friendship with you.

I didn't try to make all these lines rhyme,
It's something I've picked up, with all my spare time.
I hope to be home just as soon as I can,
Don't wait until then, to tell me where we stand.

Should I waste my stamp, should I waste my time?
Or should I just erase you from my mind?
Nothing has changed, the Earth still faces the moon,
So if you happen to think about me, "Write back soon."

Date: 05-16-1993
Location: F.C.I. Talladega
#45

DRIVE BY SHOOTINGS

From L.A. to Chicago to New York City.
Innocent kids are dying, oh what a pity.
With gun in hand, car speeding away, you just killed two strangers,
But anybody can be brave in the absence of danger.

A baby was killed and you laughed, thinking it was cute,
Whatever happened to the old ways of settling a dispute?
Six times out of ten you didn't kill the one you hunted,
Instead you killed a student all the colleges wanted.

Where did you get this idea, from watching T.V.?
Did you learn anything in school or was all your classes P.E.?
Oh, what a fool you are if you think you're gonna get away clean,
I guess nobody has told you that Hell still accepts teens.

When you think of shootings, drive-bys are in a league of their own,
When the shooter's time comes, they'll wish they never were born.
They think they're brave, but they're really cowards in a car,
Because bravery is doing something, and showing who you are.

Date: 05-17-1991
Location: F.C.I. Talladega
#46

STUCK ON STUPID

This is my view of guys doing time,
The ones building their bodies instead of their minds.
You build your body trying to look like cupid,
You don't build the mind, so you'll always be "Stuck on Stupid."

Look at your hands, then look at your feet,
They tell the truth of how you lived on the streets.
You listen to rap songs that you can't comprehend,
If you understood the message your problems could end.

Instead of the news, you love watching a movie,
To you, staying in prison is just fine and groovy.
You brag of the women you laid and the money you made,
But on fighting your case, nothing is said.

You seem happy, being in prison with all your homeboys,
You're like a little kid on Christmas, playing with his toys.
You talk a lot of trash about taking someone's life,
But you should be killed, for taking a man as your wife.

You're "Stuck on Stupid," but you're becoming a fool,
The answer to your condition is to get into school.
If you read this poem and it applies to you,
The next thing to think is, "What am I going to do?"

Date: 06-30-1993
Location: F.C.I. Talladega
#47

I'LL CRY TOMORROW

I've lived a pretty good life, but with nothing to show,
I've gone through Hell, just to know what I know.
I've traveled from city to city and state to state.
But the more I ventured, only got me closer to Hell's
gate.

I've had lots of money, now I'm without a dime to my
name,
The pursuit of all that money, only brought me shame.
I've been very happy, but now I'm full of sorrow,
Depressed so bad, that I'll put off crying until tomorrow.

I had a wife and daughter, for which I was very proud,
But lost everything I love, under the midst of a black
cloud.
I had a great job, doing something good everyday,
"That's a fine young man," the people would say.

Things were going well until in prison I arrived,
Now today, I'm worth more, dead than alive.
Your friend I was, when it was something you borrowed,
Today, I have very few friends, again, I'll cry tomorrow.

Now I sit in prison, lonely every night.,
Life without parole, what a Hell of a plight.
Was I such a bad guy to be faced with such horrors,
I've died already, so I'll cry tomorrow.

Date: 10-01-1993
Location: F.C.I. Talladega #48

I'LL GET OUT OF YOUR WAY

There comes a time in everyone's life, when one must
part,
With some of the things he loves or even cares about.
Foolish was I, to believe that you'd be with me always,
Love comes from the heart not from the mouth of what
one says.

Silly was I to think that I could depend on you time after
time,
But that's the price I have to pay for having a one track
mind.
I guess I can't complain, you was by my side for a little
while,
I must remember, I'm a grown man and not a little child.

But isn't the definition of care, "To be concerned after,"
Remember, I was there in your sadness, as well as in your
laughter.
I'm not asking you to drop everything and tend to my
needs,
I only asked that you do for me, according to my past
deeds.

Did I request too much in a visit, a few dollars or a letter?
Are you having trouble caring, now that my life is in the
cellar?
Some have written me off for dead, but I know that I'll
be back,
God will change the laws, especially the ones concerning
crack.

Here's your break, no more excuses, no more hiding and no more lying,

No more disappointing me, without even trying.

You didn't write, visit or send me money like you always say,

I'll save you the trouble of a new lie, I'll just get out of your way.

TO: MY SO-CALLED FRIENDS WHO MEANT
     TO WRITE, VISIT OR SEND MONEY,
     BUT FOUND SOMETHING ELSE TO DO.

Date: 11-08-1993
#49

Poems 50-56

WRITTEN: 12-03-1993 - 12-01-1999

INSPIRATION/BACK STORY:

Love and reflection is what this section of poems is about. I wrote very little during this six-year stretch. This was most likely the longest period for the least amount of writings. I think I was going through something.

I want people to know what I thought love was. I was reflecting back to how I had gotten to this point in my life. How I had screwed up my life so bad.

Then I thought I had fallen in love again, but I quickly realized that in prison, love is conditional. You love who loves you, even if you're not really in love with them.

Then I started to reflect on the worth of my life. I started questioning if I should even be alive. Asking God why he had me sitting and suffering, while people were dying.

LOVE IS

Love is not a game and love is not war,
Love is not anything played to keep score.
Love is not hard and cold, love is soft and warm,
Love is feeling safe, while wrapped in your arms.

Love is not tart and love is not sour,
Love is not having you on my mind from hour to hour.
Love is not bitterness, love is tender and sweet,
Love is what I have for you, and it's not discreet.

Love is not a secret, for love is to be shown,
Love is like a ring, it's made to be worn.
Love causes jealousy, love causes spite,
Love is so wonderful, when it's all done right.

Love is trusting, love is enduring and love is patience,
Love is everything when it makes any sense.
Love brings heartache, love sometimes brings pain,
But love can be as sweet as a sugar cane.

Love does to the soul, what sex does for the body,
It erases all bad feelings without making you feel sorry.
Love is not a top coat, love is very deep down,
Love comes from the heart, and not from the sound.

Love is being there for someone, when no one else
would,
Love is not questioning, whether you shouldn't or
should.
Love is a letter, because love is what you write with your
pen,

Love is always a beginning, never an end.

Love is a phone call, but it shows more in a visit,
You can't buy true love and you damn sure can't rent it.
Love is giving, when you really want to receive,
Love means to show, not to deceive.

Date: 12-03-1993
#50

MERRY CHRISTMAS SWEETHEART

This is my Christmas poem to you,
Words of happiness, so you won't feel blue.
Although, I'm not with you and we both are away,
Merry Christmas and I love you is what I want to say.

Six months ago you re-entered my life,
Before next Christmas, I pray you'll be my wife.
You know that right now I can't send you anything,
But, "I Love You Sweetheart," is what my heart will sing.

This Christmas is better than the last two I had,
Because of you, this Christmas, I won't be sad.
Christmas will pass and I will see you very soon,
You gave me my Christmas present way back in June.

Close your eyes and make a wish,
Yes, I love you sweetheart and it's you that I miss.
Now open your heart and just let me in.
And Christmas for us, will never end.

Date: 12-13-1993
#51

THE MAN IN THE MIRROR

Many mistakes in a life cut short,
I wasn't prepared for the trouble I bought.
I took a shortcut in life just to get ahead,
And I ended up someplace worse off than dead.

My mother always taught me to do what was fair,
I took a slight detour, and had a flat without a spare.
I got married, and I made promises I didn't keep,
After the divorce I started to slip in too deep.

No one made me do the things that I did,
Greed was my motivation and into a pit I slid.
I threw caution aside, and I pissed into the wind,
I reaped what I sowed, and entered the Devil's den.

I took an oath, it was "To Protect and To Serve."
Getting involved with drugs took a hell of a nerve.
I wanted to quit, but the money kept flowin',
I lost my freedom and now my life needs towing.

I woke up this morning, away from home another day,
This surely was, a hell of a price to pay.
I pray I never travel those roads again,
Because life at the top was full of sin.

Alpha is the beginning, Omega is the end,
When the wind blows hard you've got to bend.
It's sad when I think of who and where I should be,
Today I looked in the mirror, but I didn't see me.

Date: 06-12-1996 #52

NO MORE WAILING

Winning the Sugar Bowl is gonna be so sweet,
Especially when you're the Florida Gators, "The team to beat."
You beat us once, on your home field,
We're giving you 3 points again, what's the deal?

In the last game, you hit Danny Boy late on every play,
So "hell" tonight is what the Noles 'will pay.
Texas beat Nebraska, now y'all gotta meet us,
After the game, your players can cry on the team bus.

The beating you gave us the last game didn't last,
We're coming to New Orleans to kick some ass.
When the last whistle blows, a lot of money will be lost,
But through the smoke, the SEC & the Gators will be boss.

The headlines will read. "Florida State crushed by the Gators,"
Now get with the program, you player Haters.
For the next 12 months, one of these teams will be ailing,
'Cause after tonight, there's "No More Wailing."

Date: 01-01-1997
Game Played: 01-02-1997
#53

IN LOVE AGAIN

I thought life for me had ended, but you've given it a new start.
You've brought a smile to my face, and warmth to my heart.
Looking for love in all the wrong places had one hell of a cost,
For years, I thought I was happy, but I was really lost.

Now you've reentered my life and you've awakened my soul,
You're the reason why I don't feel broken; I feel whole.
It feels great knowing that you really care about me,
This time I won't let the devil blind me, so that I can't see.

Baby, one day, I'll be home and we can walk in the park,
And I will hold you in my arms as we watch the stars after dark.
You in my arms, is all that I want to hold,
I want to be your blanket when you're feeling cold.

I want to make you happy, proud, and full of joy,
I will be the only thing you need, like a child's favorite toy.
I promise to never ever leave your side,
I promise not to jump out of the car, no matter how bumpy the ride.

For the past six years, I've prayed to God for a new life.
Took him awhile, but he said you're my new wife.

The love we feel now, is stronger than before,
As each day goes by, I love you even more.

Date: 10-03-1997
#54

"TO FREE MY SOUL"

Here I am trapped in this living hell,
Can't get home, so home has to be my cell.
Everyday, it's the same thing over and over again,
Done it so much, it doesn't matter where I begin.

Surrounded everyday by idiots and knuckleheads,
The only time I feel alive, is when I go to bed.
Wake up the next day and everything is still the same,
So much wasted time, who invented this game?

Many nights I've wished that I don't wake the next day,
God didn't agree, so he woke me up anyway.
One night, as I slept, God came to me in my dreams,
Showed me my kids, and said, "It's not as bad as it
seems."

I woke up sweating, and started pacing the floor,
I thought, "That had to be a nightmare, I still can't open
this door."
I finally went back to sleep, and God appear to me once
more,
He said, "My son, Your body's here, but your Soul is
beyond the door."

Now I know what my dreams really meant,
Use the time I have now and make it well spent.
I write poetry just to get away from it all,
God was just showing me, it reveals the Soul of Julius
Hall.

"INCARCERATION TAKES THE BODY, NOT THE SOUL"

Date: 11-30-1999
#55

"I'D TAKE YOUR PLACE IF I COULD"

Have you ever sat back and wondered why,
Someone so wonderful and precious had to die?
Life is exciting and in some ways it's so sweet,
But you dying so young, makes me feel so weak.

No one likes to lose a loved one, especially a child,
Of God, she was just here for a little while.
But who are we to question, the wisdom of our maker,
We don't have that right, because he's the giver and the
taker.

Death is so strange, because it really makes you think,
Things like, "Did I take my Vitamins, A, B, C, E and the
Zinc?"
One thing for sure and that is we all must die,
But will your soul go to hell or to those "Gates in the
sky?"

Martin Luther King said, that death does not
discriminate,
So it's only objective? To terminate.
Have you known anybody to die and you would,
Say "I'd take your place, If I could?"

Death strikes everybody, the young or old, rich or poor,
Black or White,
It comes in the morning, noon, evenings and in the night.
I'm not gonna think about what I didn't do or what I
should,
Because, I'd take your place if I really could.

"DEATH ENDS A LIFE, NOT A RELATIONSHIP"

Date: 12-01-1999
#56

Poems 57-64

WRITTEN: 01-04-2000 - 07-06-2001

INSPIRATION/BACK STORY:

Ain't God good. Poems of some spiritual reflection. Six of these eight poems were written thinking about how good and amazing God is. Even the two poems I wrote to Gabrielle and Akeem, was me reflecting on God's grace to me. God didn't give me any mercy, he gave me something greater than mercy, he bestowed upon me his grace.

The grace of God will take you where the mercy of God will not. Mercy is for an instance, grace is for a period of time.

TALENT VS. HYPE

January 4th 2000 is gonna be one hell of a night,
The Hokies and Seminoles will be in a rough dog fight.
Florida State has something called, "Too much team speed,"
But when the clock runs out, points will be what they need.

Dunn is gone & Charlie Ward plays with the Knicks,
The only points they'll score will be from kicks.
Bowlware has left and the freak ends are missing,
The Championship trophy is what the Hokies will be kissing.

Weinke will be on his back all over the field,
Hardly any points will Cory Moore yield.
Bobby B. will jump up & down, and scream & holler,
That was just the first half, two more quarters to follow.

The Hokies are very good on their special teams,
Blocking punts and kick off returns straight down the seams.
On defense, we have Moore, Charlton, Williams & Midget,
Peter Warrick running wild & loose? , Forget about it.

Seminoles fans across the county will be sick,
Especially when the MVP trophy, is handed to Michael Vick.
Stud on suicide watch? No he's not the type.
But he should've known, it was V.T. Talent vs FL. St. Hype.

Date: 12-08-1999
Game Date: 01-04-2000
#57

"TO AKEEM"

Son, I'm sorry I wasn't there when you needed me most,
I'm sorry I wasn't there at breakfast, to butter your toast.
I'm sorry I wasn't there on your first day of school.
But I wish I was there to advise you of the rules.

I'm sorry I wasn't there when you hit the winning shot,
But I was there in Spirit, this, please don't doubt.
I'm sorry I wasn't there to take you to the park,
I'm sorry I wasn't there when you called out in the dark.

I'm sorry I wasn't there to play "Throw and Catch,"
Sorry I wasn't there to fill the hole you needed patched.
Sorry I wasn't there to take you to the boys club,
I'm especially sorry, I wasn't there to show you my love.

Akeem, I'm sorry I wasn't there to show you what roads
to follow,
Sorry I wasn't there to tie your tie and fix your shirt
collar.
I'm sorry I wasn't there to pick you up when you fell,
Sorry, I wasn't there, to show you your sister, Gabrielle.

I'm sorry I wasn't there to be the first to call you
"Keemie,"
Son, I'm sorry I wasn't there for you to truly get to know
"me."
And son, I'm sorry I was a father, considered "missing in
action,"

But you're still my son, although we had no interaction.

Date: 12-28-2000
#58

"TO GABRIELLE"

Baby, I'm sorry I wasn't there to hold you when you were scared,
I'm sorry I wasn't there to back you when you were dared.
I'm sorry I wasn't there to read you bedtime stories at night,
But I promise I'll spend the rest of my life making it right.

The day you were born, I was a very happy man,
You've never disappointed me, and you never ever can.
I'm sorry I didn't get to be at your first piano recital,
I hope that you don't think that "Father," shouldn't be my title.

I'm sorry I wasn't in church on the day that you sung,
But I can tell you, I was smiling all week long.
I'm sorry I wasn't there to teach you tennis and volleyball,
But you'll do just fine, after all, you are a Hall.

I'm sorry I wasn't there to attend your P.T.A. meetings,
I'm sorry I wasn't there to answer all your pleadings.
I'm sorry I wasn't 'there when you went on your first date,
But I wish I was there to talk, when you stayed out too late.

You're growing up now, turning out just as I'd hope,

There's nothing in this world for which you can not cope.

So reach for the stars and if you land on the moon, that's good too,

But know this, daddy's got your back, and I'd die for you.

Gabrielle, Although I'm not there, we'll always have each other,

I'm not only your daddy, I'm your big brother.

If you never find that someone to make them a good wife,

Don't worry too much, 'cause you're already the love of my life.

Date: 12-28-2000

#59

"THINK ABOUT IT"

Have you ever thought about all the wonders of the
world?
Deep thought on this subject makes my mind swirl.
Like, how does an aspirin know where to go to stop the
pain?
And who was the person who thought of the sewage
drain?

How does a clock know how to keep the exact time?
Whose thought was money, the dollar, the quarter, nickel
and dime?
How does a microwave know how to cook your foods?
And how does Prozac know how to control your moods?

How is a telephone able to carry someone's voice?
What's this about an abortion pill, that gives you a
choice?
One of the smartest things lately is the invention of the
Internet,
But do you believe in being intimate with someone
you've never met?

And what's spying on us morning, noon and at night?
Big, huge, powerful cameras above us, called satellites.
What's these voices on a "Radio" of people I can't see?
And whose these people on the box, everyone calls a
T.V.?

Who invented the alphabets for the words that we speak?
And who knows the exact location of the God we all
seek?

Atomic bombs can take millions of lives before you can blink,
But you have the ability, to control how you think.

Date: 01-01-2000
#60

"BUSHWHACKED IN FLORIDA"

The 2000 Election was one Hell of a mess,
They didn't count every vote so they had to guess.
We had pregnant Chads and the clearly punched hanging
Chads.
Overvotes, undervotes, it nearly drove me and Al Gore
mad.

Every week, for 7 weeks, there was a new issue before
the court,
Before one could be resolved, CNN had another to
report.
When the spin began, Gore had Christopher, Bush had
Jim Baker,
One looked like a drunk, and the other, a cemetery care-
taker.

Then in came the lawyers, Bush with Richard, Gore with
Boise,
Two clever attorneys, never losing their poise.
Each, in the long 7 weeks, would argue good points of
law,
But when the U.S Supreme Court ruled, it left me with a
hanging jaw.

Democrats and Republicans squared off and traded
shoves and pushes,
While Jesse Jackson was in the middle warning, "Stay out
of the Bushes."
The Florida Supremes did twice, what I thought to be
fair,
Bush didn't trust the people, so he sought the U.S.

Supremes 'care.

Enter three more judges, Sauls, Lewis and the wise Nikki Clark,
They took us on a roller coaster ride around the block.
The lawyers were in rare form, especially David Boise.
But in the very end, the U.S, Supremes made the most noise.

When they were finished, they had stuck a knife in Al Gore,
But it's just a flesh wound Al, we'll be back stronger in 2004.
I listened to Greta, Bernie, Jeff, Wolf and even Roger Cossack,
But when it was all over, I knew that, I had just been Bushwacked.

Date: 01-01-2000
#61

IMAGINE THAT

Ever wondered how an airplane is able to stay in the sky?
Have you ever wondered why things with wings, are the
only things to fly?
Or how a huge ship is able to stay on the ocean and
float?
And how is a submarine able to dive under, or sail like a
boat?

Who invented this thing we know as an X-Ray machine?
And who invented the color camera, that can copy
everything seen?
Who invented the tape recorder, that can play back what
someone says?
And whose thought is the calendar, that numbers our
days?

Who invented eyeglasses, to make your vision much
clearer?
Whose thought was the microscope, that brings things
once unseen nearer?
Whose idea was toilet paper, to clean yourself after
you're
through?
And who invented the bath soap, that makes you feel
clean and brand new?

Whose idea was the toothbrush, and it's cleaner the
toothpaste?
Used together, they can remove stains, without leaving a
trace.
Who invented the bicycle, and who inspired Ford to

make the car?
And who put together the telescope, to see things from afar?

Who invented the system for purifying our water?
Whose thought was the police, to keep our society in order?
Sit back and imagine these things if you can,

But the most amazing thing ever, was God's invention of man.

Date: 01-11-2001
#62

A PRAYER FROM ME

Oh Lord, Thank you for watching over me during the night,
Thank you, Oh Lord, for making my heavy burdens feel so light.
I want to thank you Lord, for my son, my daughters and my mom,
I thank you Lord for my wisdom, as well as my charm.

I want to thank you Lord for my abilities to discern,
Thank you Lord for the last 10 years of what I've learned.
Thank you, Oh Lord, for the tears that I've cried.
Thank you Lord for showing me life, just when I thought I had died.

Thank you Lord, for all the new true friends that I've made,
Some closer than family, I have no fear of being betrayed.
Thank you Father for showing me, how to do things your way,
Thank you Father for controlling, the things that I say.

Lord, I thank you for my skills and for my ability to understand,
Please bless me for my unselfishness, and my willingness to lend a hand.
Lord, I thank you for my abilities to hear, smell, feel and to see,
I thank you Lord for redirecting my life, and for creating me.

Lord, all I'm asking for now is another chance at life,
A chance to be a good servant, father, son, and husband
to my wife.
Lord, I ask these things from the very depth of the faith
that I hold,
I need your help Lord, so please come to my aid, and
rescue my soul.

Date: 01-22-2001
#63

AIN'T GOD GOOD?

God is good, that's one thing I surely know,
He's been directing my life, even if it does not show.
He's not good some of the time, he's good all the time,
God doesn't have to sway on that very thin line.

God wakes me up and he also causes me to sleep,
God is the reason I laugh, God is the reason I weep.
Whenever I think about all the Hell I'm going through,
He shows me what I have, this time he showed me you.

Things I thought I'd lost forever, are showing up in my
face,
God is the doer of all things, he's the creator of my
grace.
God knows my thoughts, my secrets and everyone of my
needs.
He is my healer, whenever my soul bleeds.

When the Earth is too dry, it is God that causes the rain,
When my heart was broken, it was God who eased my
pain.
God is the reason for the air that we breathe,
Minds focused on God, is what we all should heed.

God is the reason we have the day and the night,
He's also the reason to run from wrong, and walk into
right.
Miracles happen everyday, and we make them such a big
deal,
That's God just showing us, not to guess if he's real.

AIN'T GOD GOOD?

Date: 07-06-2001
#64

Poems 65-74

WRITTEN: 07-16-2001 - 11-20-2001

INSPIRATION/BACK STORY:

Love, love, love. 10 poems on love and what I was going through. I guess I'm just a hopeful romantic. I love being in love. Three things you chase all your life are money, God and love.

I went through every phase of love, the lows, the highs and the in betweens. Lucky is the woman that gets this love. Blessed is the woman who can harness and keep it.

NO ME WITHOUT YOU

The sweetest thing to come out of Sugartown is you,
And for the rest of your life, you'll forever be my boo.
Your smile can melt the hardest of any heart,
Your kindness is what won me over from the start.

For ten long years I've felt empty, from the lack of you,
The moment I found you, is when I began life anew.
They say that life cannot be sustained, without the drink
of water,
But without you in mine's, was the worst of all disorders.

You are and always was, the object of my desire,
You are my drug and I want to get higher.
I can do without food, water and every other care,
But me without you is like space without air.

Continue the life you have, because it seems to be steady,
But the minute I touch down, you'd better be ready.
I can do without "her", and your life, he cannot make,
But me without you, is like Superman without his cape.

A seed needs to be planted before anything can grow,
A book is to be read, and true love always shows.
Just like Batman needs Robin, and a large ship needs the
sea,
My dear sweetheart, without you, there certainly is no me.

Date: 07-16-2001
#65

REAL LOVE, DEEP LOVE, TRUE LOVE

Being in love can make you feel like you're going crazy,
If you have it bad like me, it can make you feel lazy.
Real love can make you feel like you're walking on a
cloud,
Deep love can make you shout it out loud.

True love, will have you up in the wee hours of the night,
True love, makes you tremble when your lover is in sight.
Deep love will have you playing Luther and some Pattie
Labelle,
Deep love is a love you can't rent, buy or sell.

Real love makes you feel like you've never ever felt
before,
It'll change your other plans, and make them very unsure.
Deep love will have you thinking, of the one you love all
day long,
It'll make your knees buckle, when you finally get them in
your arms.

True love will make your lover, the only object to be
adored,
It'll also make everyone and everything else, objects to be
ignored.
Real love and True love can never grow tired or old,
Deep love is so powerful, it'll make you warm, when it's
freezing cold.

Deep love has me walking around all day, with you on
my mind,

I've lost track of almost everything, even the time.
Any kind of love will have you waiting by the phone,
But one of these three loves, will make you feel it in your
bones.

Date: 07-30-2001
#66

MY PROMISE TO YOU

I promise to give you my undivided attention,
I promise that our love will defy a definition.
I promise to think of no other love but yours,
I promise that you'll have the keys, to unlock all my closed doors.

I promise to taste no kiss, but from your lips,
I promise that my hands will touch, only your waist and your hips.
I promise that the passion I feel for you will never fade,
I promise that if the sun gets too hot, I'll be your shade.

I promise that my heart will beat every beat only for you,
I promise to include you, in everything I do.
I promise to never let anything come between our love,
I promise the only thing that can, is an order from above.

I promise that you'll never be kept in the dark,
I promise to guard our love, and give it it's spark.
I promise that every step I take up, you'll be by my side,
I promise to remind the world, you're the reason for my rise.

I promise to never ever cause you, any days of pain,
I promise to be your umbrella, if you're ever caught in the rain.
I promise to hold you, to love you and to never let you go,
I promise to stand in front of you, no matter how hard the wind blows.

I promise that besides God, the only other thing I'll worship is you,

I promise when I say, "I truly love you," It'll only be for you too.

I promise that you are and always will be, the love of my life,

I promise no matter how long it takes, I'm gonna make you my wife.

Date: 07-31-2001
#67

FOREVER MINE

You are my first, you are my last,
You are the one that makes my heart beat so fast.
I need you now, more than ever before,
You give me love and so much more.

Sometimes I cry, When I think of you,
Not cause I'm hurt, but from all that we've made it
through.
You mean the world to me, this I can't ignore,
The love we share, has so much in store.

You mean so much to me right now,
No greater love will ever be found.
I can't explain in words what you do to me,
But our love will forever be a part of history.
I only say the things I say and do,
Because I'll forever love you, and you'll always be my
"Pooh."

Written By: Gabrielle D. Hall
Date: 05-01-2001
#68

LOVE HURTS

There's a pain in my head, and my legs are shaking,
I haven't heard from her, and now my heart is aching.
It's only been seven days, but I've got this feeling in my
gut,
Something's on the chopping block, it's my head, my
butt.

Ten years ago, I promised myself to never again love this
deep,
Now I'm hurting so bad, I wish I'd die in my sleep.
All day long and I can think of nothing but her,
Can't focus on anything else, everything's a blur.

I haven't eaten much since the last day we talked,
Planes flying into buildings, then out of my life she
walked.
Changed the phone number, and didn't even think to
drop me a letter,
But she's still loved the same, as the first day I met her.

I can't sleep, I keep waking in the middle of the night,
Her love slipped away, because I wasn't there to hold it
tight.
Just like life, love is a very, very powerful force,
But for me, love is my curse, and its punishment is
divorce.

I know for a fact, that she really is my soulmate,
Without her in my life, the only thing I'll know is hate.

If you see her before me, Please tell her where she's at on my meter,
If I see her first, I'll tell her just how much I need her.

LOVE HURTS!

Date: 09-18-2001
#69

A FOOL FOR LOVE

I always took pride in being a problem solver,
Now I'm the one confused, how's that for being novel?
I go to bed early, because I can't stand to be woke,
I wake throughout the night, because my heart is broke.

I've fallen and I can't get up, powerless to this thing I
seek,
I'm stronger than this, but lately, love has me feeling so
weak.
I'm like a sixteen year old, going thru a puppy love phase,
This hurt is penetrating my soul, and it's showing on my
face.

Hope is the engine, that drove my love for you,
Hopelessness is my "Titanic," which has me feeling so
blue.
I need something to help me ease all this pain,
I need to hear her voice, or I'll soon go insane.

Of all the feelings, why do I feel like I was betrayed?
Why do I feel like the faithful lover, who just got played?
I learned a lesson, and I guess I got exactly what I
deserved,
But never again, will anybody ever kick me to the curb.

A black cloud is following me, I can't break it's hold,
No wonder why my world suddenly feels, so lonesome
and cold.
I've become a fool for love all over again,
If I get up this time, this is where it ends.

LET ME KNOW

For twenty years, we've been sneaking and running around,
Now I'm up to the plate, but there's no pitcher on the mound.
For twenty years, we've loved each other from the very first day,
But how much longer do we have to hide our love this way?

First, you waited on me, and now I sit here waiting on you,
We were never free at the same time, so what could we do?
But sweetheart, we're getting older, and I'm growing tired,
We need to be together completely, before our time expires.

There's decisions to make, and someone's feelings will be torn,
I'm tired of hiding our love, it is time for it to be worn.
Baby let me know, when you're finished doing your part,
Let me know if there's a day, when our new life can truly start.

When you take this step, there is no turning back,
So pull the rope tight, there's no room for any slack.
Once you're out, take some time to see if I'm what you want,
Then let me know, whether you truly do or you don't.

I need to know so that I can set goals, and make new plans,

So let me know the person's name, who will be your right hand?

For all of my life, I've always been number one,
But you need to let me know, if this is a race that can be won?

Date: 10-11-2001

#71

WHEN A MAN CRIES

Is it okay when a man sheds some tears?
Or is he considered weak amongst his peers?
What should it take to make a man want to cry?
Should it be death, poverty, loneliness or a love he was denied?

I cry most times when I bend down in heavy prayer,
It's like having a headache, crying becomes my Bayer.
I cry when I go to bed, and you're not there with me at night,
I cry when it's total darkness in my life, and you refuse to bring light.

I cried the day my freedom was taken away from me,
And I'm sure I'll cry again, on the day that I'm finally set free.
Love makes me cry, more than any other thing that exists,
Love makes me cry, because I love without the thought of the risks.

When a man cries and prays, it lifts a burden off his shoulders,
Because if he kept it locked inside, he'd age 40 years older.
So don't call it a weakness, when you see that this man cries,
Sensitivity lives, but the hate and bitterness within him dies.

Some might call him, just another crying fool,

But the tears soften the heart, so that it could be used as a tool.
It is said, that love is just a psychological disease,
But crying eases the pain, it is the medicine that you need.

Date: 11-13-2001
#72

AM I WORTH IT

Can you stay loyal to me for the rest of my years?
Or do I have to worry about you, with all the HIV fears?
Am I worth the drive it takes for you to come visit?
Am I worth the kisses we've shared, or do you even miss
it?

Am I worth the look I see in your eyes when we are
together?
Am I worth the times that we shared, or our promises of
forever?
Am I worth the tears I've caused to run down your face?
Am I worth you being lonely, or will someone take my
place?

Am I worth the ink that it takes to write me a letter?
Am I worth the hugs we shared that was as warm as a
sweater?
Am I worth the "I love you's," that echoes from your
sweet lips?
Or is this my last strike and you're preparing my pink
slip?

Am I worth the headaches I've caused you and all the
other pains?
Am I worth the breakdown you've had? Am I driving
you insane?
Am I worth the money you'd spend, coming to visit a
fool like me?
Am I worth the time you spent, trying to find out what in
me you see?

Am I worth the value you'd bring to my life, in the form of stability?

Or am I worth the toll I've put you through, in my letters of hostility?

Are you going to quit this easy on me, while I'm stuck in a pit?

Or are you going to evaluate our history, to see if I'm really worth it?

Date: 11-14-2001
#73

LOVES MYSTERY

Love is a most splendid thing indeed,
Love is what we want, love is what we need.
Love for me, is so very easy to find,
Holding on to it, is what boggles my mind.

Love always puts itself, in a position for me to reach out
and feel it,
But I'm not patient enough, I always try to steal it.
If you want a good man, there's none better than me on
this planet,
But don't make the mistake, of taking my absence for
granted.

I thought I knew it, but I guess I really don't,
I thought I had all the answers, but I can't figure out
what it wants.
I was always told, "Aim high and reach for the stars."
But I ran out of fuel, and I feel stranded alone on Mars.

With love, you have to be able, to see without opening
your eyes,
You have to be able to feel in the dark, to sort through its
lies.
Love will let you chase it, knowing that it's elusive,
It'll even let you catch it, fooling you into feeling
exclusive.

So never chase something ,that does not want to be
caught,
And never second guess, what's really in your heart.

Because love is right in front of me, but it, I can not grab,
The thing I want most in this world, is the thing I cannot
have.

Date: 11-20-2001
#74

Poems 75-86

WRITTEN: 02-25-2003 - 10-28-2022

INSPIRATION/BACK STORY:

Feeling abandoned, the last section of my writings deal with people coming back and forth in my life. Remember, I was in prison during this time. I came home February 2013. For 21.5 years, I had to be strong, because strong was the only option that I had that made sense. They threw me into the wolves den, but I came back leading the pack. They threw me into the devil's fire pit, but God wouldn't let the flames burn me. Thus, began the journey of the lion's roar.

FEELING ALONE IN THIS WORLD

I went to the telephone, but I didn't feel like talking,
I went to the walking track, but I didn't feel like walking.
I sat in front of the T.V. to watch a main sporting event,
I couldn't sit still, there was so much I needed to vent.

I laid down in bed and had a very mysterious dream,
I dreamt of love, freedom and friends, things that aren't
what they seem.
In this dream, my life passes by me, but it's hard to get a
description.
It looked so sad and hopeless, I think it needs a
prescription.

Abandoned and forgotten, don't know how much longer
I can cope,
Walked on and lied to, someone please throw me a bottle
of hope.
I feel alone in this world, without any hope and very little
inspiration,
Prayer, faith and my kids; are my only real motivations.

Can't do anything right and nothing wants to work itself
out.
I feel like a fish out of water, how did I get this hook in
my mouth?
Today, for some reason, I feel like a motherless child,
All alone in this world, I pray that it's not for too long a
while.

Woke up this morning, but feeling the same as I did

when I went to bed,

Got down on my knees to pray and to ask God, "Why I'm not yet dead?"

He said, because I'm his fine gem, his rare diamond, and his exquisite pearl,

He said, son, I woke you up to show you, you're not alone in this world.

Date: 02-25-2003
#75

YOU'LL SEE ME AGAIN

I can remember back just a few years ago,
That I was there for you, when you have nowhere to go.
I remember giving you just about anything I had,
I even helped carry the casket, when we buried your dad.

There was hardly ever a time, when it was me that needed
you,
But when you called on me, there was nothing I wouldn't
do.
Now I'm down on my luck, barely able to stand on my
own,
I didn't add it up, but I threw you more than a few
bones.

I know that I am responsible for whatever happens to
me,
But who was there to help me, with those things I did
not see?
Yes, I am the one who got myself into this jam,
So I can't hold you accountable, for who I now am.

When I got arrested, I didn't tell what you were doing,
Even though they were hot on my tracks, like a pot of
coffee brewing.
But life has a way of slowing everything down,
You can go from the top to the bottom at the speed of
sound.

I didn't ask in my life, for you to re-enter,
But since you have, there's been no summer, only winter.

I really do appreciate the little things you did do,
But the thing I hate most in this world, is being lied to.

A visit, a phone call, a letter, just something to keep me
warm,
Instead of lies, excuses, attitudes and a violent storm.
The one that walks in when the world walks out, is called
a friend,
Think you've seen the last of me? I promise, you'll see
me again.

TO EVERYONE THAT'S BEEN IN MY LIFE BUT
ISN'T NOW,
FRIENDS, LOVERS, FAMILY, EX-WIVES, YOU
KNOW WHO YOU ALL ARE….

Date: 05-13-2003
#76

MY SEARCH FOR YOU

Looking for someone to love, but I can't find a soul.
Looking for someone to hug, but there's not one to hold.
Looking for someone to care, but everyone walked out.
Looking for someone to talk to, to tell all my problems about.

Looking for someone to listen to, but no one wants to talk.
Looking for someone to hold my hand, on this long journey I must walk.
Looking for someone to forgive me, for all the wrong I did over the years.
Looking for someone to say they understand, when I fall to my knees in tears.

Looking for someone to believe in me, when my dreams to them I reveal.
Looking for someone to trust me, when it's only love that I want to steal.
Looking for someone to be thinking of me, day after day after day.
Looking for someone to hear me, even when I have nothing to say.

Looking for someone to pick me up, when to the ground I fall.
Looking for someone to hold me down, when my ego grows too tall.
Looking for someone to show concern, when the world don't give a damn.
Looking for someone to smile with me, and accept me

for who I am.

Looking for someone to advise me, to help make me all
that I can be.
Looking for someone to share my life, on still waters or
on rough seas.
Looking for someone to cry with me, for these heavy
burdens I carry alone.
Looking for someone to laugh with me, when the sun
shines after this storm.

Date: 05-17-2004
#77

WHERE WERE YOU?

Where were you, when the flame went out in my life?
Where were you, when my moon didn't shine and my
sun wouldn't give light?
Where were you, when all I felt like I wanted to do was
die?
Where were you, when all I did every weekend was cry?

Where were you, when to my name not a penny did I
have?
Where were you, when I got in too deep and needed
someone to pay my tab?
Where were you, when I called your house over and over
the other day?
Where were you, when total triple darkness fell my way?

Where were you, when from the depth of my soul, I
called out your name?
Where were you, when I needed to be comforted after
my shame?
Where were you, when I needed to see just one friendly
face?
Where were you, when I lost everything and was
disgraced?

Where were you, when not one letter did I get in the
mail?
Where were you, when satan had my soul trapped in his
jail?
Where were you, when I was begging for you to show me
love?
Where were you, were you out dancing in some

nightclub?

Where were you, when my world was consumed with fire?

Where were you, when I needed to hear a song from the choir?

Where were you, when I needed to hear honey, baby, sugar, or I love you?

Where were you, please tell me, where in the hell were you?

Date: 06-01-2004
#78

THINKING OF YOU

Just like a memory, I can't seem to get you out of my head,
Just like a hurricane's aftermath, I see our relationship is in shreds.
I've done everything I can, to erase you from my mind,
But I can't handle the rain, or any day the sun does not shine.

Why I still love you, is what really teases my brain,
But it's days like today, I really can't stand the rain.
Everytime I call a friend, I can't help but to ask about you,
But you've moved on with your life, why do I still care what you do?

Love is a sickness, a disease, for which there is only one cure.
And that is to find someone else to love, Someone to make me feel secure.
But you're on my mind at least twenty of a day's twenty-four hours,
I'm thinking about you at work, at play, but especially in the shower.

I guess I still need something solid from you to hold onto,
I just wish you would give me a reason, to make me believe in you.
I wanted to call you today, just so I could hear your voice,

But I hung up the phone when I realized, I had made the wrong choice.

So I got a pen and pad to write you a very long letter,
Then I remembered, I express myself in poetry, a little bit
better.
As I was sitting there writing and thinking only about you,
I stopped to say a prayer, wishing that you were thinking about me too.

Date: 04-21-2005
#79

TEARS AND PRAYERS

Alone by myself, I finally got a chance to cry today,
Because I wanted to feel, what my soul had to say.
I just needed to shed some of those soulful tears,
Two years without crying, too many reasons, too many
fears.

I couldn't cry in front of my friends, I would've lost their
respect,
I was the leader, the organizer, the man, so what did I
expect?
Where was I then, in the open, it was always someone in
my face,
Where I'm at now, In confinement, I can cry with no
thought of disgrace.

Everyday, they'd see me, I'd have a smile on my face and
a demeanor that said, "Strong as can be,"
But little did they know, the pressure, the time, and the
loneliness, was killing me.
I really just needed to cry my heart out today,
I hope God was listening, because I really had a lot to
say.

I've never been able to cry, without also saying a prayer,
That's always when I needed God the most, and I knew
that he'd be there.
While I'm talking to God, I'm free from all my other
concerns.
I put everything in his hands, and then the next page I
turn.

I've lost so many things over the last 16 years.
Being hurt so bad, I know I've cried a bathtub full of tears.
Lord thank you for letting me cry out loud to you today,
Because if I couldn't, I feel like I just wanted to die today.

Date: 12-02-2005

#80

POKER WITH THE DEVIL

The Devil came up from Hell with his pitch fork in his
hand,
He interrupted our card game, stating that he was looking
for a good man.
All of a sudden, six guys jumped up, all seemingly in a
rush,
Until I said, "Sit yall ass down, nobody's leaving, when I
got a straight flush."

The Devil said, "I'll pay you twice the amount of that
pot,
cause all money is the same."
Then I said, "Excuse me Satan, But your ass wasn't even
invited to this game.?
I told him, "So sit your ass down or back the Hell away
from my table."
'Cause if I have to tell your ass this again, after that you
won't be able.

The Devil got mad and said, "Do you know who I am?
I've got killers in my stable."
I said, "Well I suggest you call them motherfuckers, or
move on to the Dominos table."
Nobody moved,so the Devil said, "Damn son, you've got
a lot of power",
I said, "I don't care what you think I've got, I'm loosing,
and this game is over in an hour".

The Devil jumped on top of the table, but slipped on a
chip and landed on his butt,

My partner got mad and slapped the shit out of the Devil, cause he was holding up the cut.

He said to Satan, "Bitch sit your ass down, the game will be over soon."

If you interrupt this game one more time, I'll skin your ass like a coon.

The Devil then said, "Do y'all know, the only one who can defeat me is God?"

Then the whole table told him, "You'll know different if you don't allow us to deal the cards.

The Devil walked out mumbling, "Damn these poker players are tough."

The poker players were all relieved, that Satan had fallen for their bluff.

Date: 12-03-2005

#81

TODAY, TOMORROW, & FOREVER

I don't know what forces drove you to come my way,
But I've learned not to question fate, I'll just pray that
you stay.
Life sometimes deals you hands, that you don't want to
play,
Good hands don't come along often, so you must live for
today.

It's hard to find someone you can talk to, about any and
everything.
Someone that makes you look forward, to what
tomorrow might bring.
Relationships can have your emotions going from
happiness to sorrow,
I'll take what we have right now, instead of having to
search for tomorrow.

Love is something, that can have you walking on the
clouds,
It will make you go to the mountain top, and declare it
out loud.
So when the love bug comes, try not to think the word
"never,"
Love tells the heart, that what you're feeling is forever.

When our eyes meet, there's a smile that comes across
your face,
It says that no one else matters, in the entire human race.
Yes, I'd like to mold you, but you can still do as you may,
I'm thinking for our future, and not only for today.

Your willingness to change those things, you know to be bad,

Your saying, "I'll do that for you baby," without ever getting mad.
These things and more, makes loving you seem so smart and clever,

So I'll cherish your gift of love to me, today, tomorrow and forever.

Date: 08-13-2006
#82

STRAIGHT UP, NO CHASER

I cannot help myself, I just say exactly what I Feel.
I believe the people deserve a voice, especially one that is Real.
Not being afraid and making things as plain as they can Be.
Speaking Truth to Power, like Alicia Miller Blakely.

The people voted you in, on a promise that you would be their Voice.
Being on the side of the people, that should be your only Choice.
Fighting for the people, without ever having to Barter.
Being "Not For Sale." like Kesha Gibson-Carter.

The Bartow property gives us all, a reason to Weep.
Elected officials, you all have, a Charge to Keep.
We respect our leaders more when they show no Fear.
Speak up and say it boldly, like Bernetta Lanier.

Getting things done, we should be people of Action.
Striving to be just like, State Senator Lester Jackson.
Rising above the foolishness and still throwing a Blow.
Strong & young new leaders, like Derek Mallow.

Saying what is necessary, means no one gets a free Pass,
Knowing the rules of the game like Dr. Estella Shabazz.
Engaging the people everyday, is what we love to See.
It's all about the Community, to Councilman Thomas Barbee.

The future of our children, is what really matters to us

All.

We are lucky to have a Servant, like Dr. Tonia Howard-Hall.

The History of our people is why we need Dr. Jamal Toure'.

Memories passed down and preserved, hooray, hooray, Hooray.

A Politician serves themselves, while a Servant serves the People.

We need to vet the right persons, and start labeling them "Keepers."

Don't make promises to the people, and later use an Eraser.

I like my Truth told direct, Straight Up, No Chaser.

Date: 04-19-2021

#83

THAT ASS GOT SPANKED

Tonight, I am eating steak while Jodi and Linda is eating Crow.

 He didn't believe me, but the people said, "Incumbents Had To Go."

Jodi and Adam thought they could influence voters, so they took to Facebook to Cry.
Everything that came out their mouths smelled like a Lie.

Jodi sent out an email predicting the winners like he's Nostradamus,
When really all he is, is a Redneck Dumbass.

Adam took a break from warming hotdogs between his Jaws
And went out to hold signs in tight jeans, and had on no Drawers.

Linda couldn't wait so she ran to the gym before the Votes were finished being Counted.
At 9pm she looked Like a mule that couldn't be Mounted.

Linwood got 4 more votes than the last time he ran and Lost.
But in the end, finishing 3rd does not make you a Boss, his ass got Tossed.

Gary saw the numbers and blocked all incoming Calls.
He couldn't face Linda because he didn't have any Balls.
Jodi's keyboard seems to now be missing some Keys.

He has not sent council any emails, with his demands and his Pleas.

Brenda Boulware isn't laughing anymore with that ugly ass Smile.
Looking like a rat in the face, with no class or Style.

Jimmy and Shonta were seen at City Hall working late in the Day.
Were they shredding files, or updating their Resumes?

Libby was last seen hauling ass out of Town.
He was late to a job interview, because he doesn't know how much longer he'll be Around.

Jodi was last seen with his gun, loading a round into the Chamber.
Hope he shoots himself in the head, and do us all a Favor.

Adam was last seen looking for a new home in Pooler.
His last words were, "it's about to get too hot in this City, maybe Pooler is Cooler."

Alfonso was last seen, calling everyone to congratulate them on their Wins.
Then he headed out the door for church, to ask for forgiveness for his Sins.

Date: 11-04-2021
#84

THE JOURNEY: YOU KNOW HALF OF MY STORY

There were people close to me conspiring to take me out.
They underestimated my will, my strength and what
God's assignment for me was about.

The devil couldn't kill me, for if he could, I'd already be
dead.
I'm a believer in God, and I've been following what he
said.

My mom didn't spoil her kids, by sparing us the rod.
Every day in our house, was a lecture about the
Goodness of God.

Struggles, Pain and Heartache, but none of it was meant
to last.
Grateful for the lows of my life, it allowed me to shed
that shameful mask.

Many days I called out, "Oh God, if only you'd send me
a sign,"
God told me, "it's only Satan playing tricks with your
mind."

I'm not your intellectual equal, but I am your IQ
inspiration.
Unshakable, unraveled, unfazed, unafraid, I'm God's
creation.

I don't look like what I've been through, many times I've

been bested.

Oh, but look at me now, a lion roaring in the jungle, I'm battle-tested.

Should have been dead by now, but I'm covered by his Grace.
This Journey is not a sprint, it's more like a marathon race.

So some folks look at me now, in all of my glory.
But they don't know, my absolute entire story.

Twenty one years, trapped in the belly of a vicious beast.
God whispered in my ear, "wake up, the sun still rises in the east."

It's not about the path I took, or how I was raised.
If you don't know my Journey, you won't understand my praise.

Date: 10-22-2022
#85

A SHATTERED DREAM

I've revealed my whole life and my soul to you,
I've jumped over mountains and dug for gold for you.
Your soft voice, your bedroom eyes and your beautiful
smile,
I loved every moment spent with you, although it was
just for a little while.

The curve of your body, and the tenderness of your kiss,
I'm sorry that all of this, I now have to miss.
The way you called me Sweetheart, Honey & Baby,
The hope of one day calling you mine's, stopping all the
maybes.

Just being with you, would brighten up my worst kind of
day,
Making me feel better, without me having a word to say.
I've never been disappointed, with our times in between
the sheets,
Over and over and over again, my desire did you meet.

You're sensitive, sensual and most of all sexy.
You were the apple of my eye, my BFF, my bestie.
I don't know why you mistook my love, as me
controlling your life.
Every moment away from you, are moments filled with
strife.

Went to bed, but couldn't sleep or even catch a nap,
I have to find a way back to you, could you please send
me the map?

When my phone rings, I answer it quickly, hoping it's you on my ear set,

When it's not, I feel like I'm outside in the rain, without an umbrella getting soaked and wet.

Four words I didn't want to hear you say was, "I'll figure it out."

Tore my heart to pieces, I'm in Love without a doubt.

The last thing you said to me, "you will always be my friend."

Those are just code words for, "The Beginning Of The End."

Date: 10-28-2022
#86

About the Author

Julius Hall is a man of Love, of Commitment, of Dedication and Determination. He grew up in the projects and neighborhoods of West Savannah. After graduating High School, he began working at the Savannah Police Department and quickly changed course and joined the ranks of professional law enforcement officers. After 9.5 years he fell off the train and ended up getting caught up in an illegal family drug operation. Sentenced to life in 1991, but given his life back in 1997, and being released from federal prison in 2013, this is the life of a man you wouldn't believe unless you saw it in the movies. From a prison cell to his own boardroom. From being given orders to by prison guards, to celebrating events with them in the free world. From taking orders, to being the boss. From 12 cents an hour to 6 figures per year. This is the poetry to explain the in-between years. The before and after books are forthcoming, Crossing the Line: The Julius Hall Story, has already been written, but not released. Life After Life: Rebuilding Julius Hall, is being written now. And, Prison Stories: The Collaboration, is a book of great poetry and short stories by some of the best writers in America. You can go anywhere from wherever you are right now, these books will show you that. Get ready to cry, laugh, love and live the experience.

Made in the USA
Columbia, SC
13 November 2023

25901231R00102